Write for charity

How to write effectively
for your charity's marketing,
publications and website

ngo.media

Write for charity

How to write effectively for your charity's marketing, publications and website

© ngo.media ltd

Additional material: Jennifer Campbell, Matt Chittock, Barney Jeffries, Sarah Myers and Trina Wallace.

A catalogue record for this book is available from the British Library.

ISBN: 978-0-9553695-2-0

Contents

Introduction

Words are among your charity's most effective tools for inviting sympathy, changing minds, inspiring action and, vitally, generating support and donations.

And the best thing about words is that they are completely free.

In this easy-to-use book, I've pulled together nearly 150 snippets of advice that I know will help your charity produce writing, publications, media work and marketing that gets results. You can read it cover to cover, or simply dip in when you need an inspiration boost.

I concentrate on the actual writing, how to construct words, publications and online copy that will make a quick and easy difference to your organisation.

I've left strategy, debate and the latest ever-changing internet tools out of the picture. The latter would be out of date even before the ink was dry.

You'll find much more of that on our website, where you can add your own thoughts and advice.

There's always so much more to learn about great charity writing. I hope you'll continue to exercise your writing muscle after getting started with me.

To improve your writing you must learn from other writers, have your work criticised by others, read as much as you can and write as often as possible.

I hope you find the book useful and good luck with the work.

Gideon Burrows
ngo.media
www.ngomedia.org.uk

The basics

Getting your readers' attention

START WHERE THE ACTION IS

The Children's Health Trust has been awarded £300,000 from the Treegreen Foundation, to assist its work with young people in deprived areas. The funding will provide places for hundreds of children to go on adventure weekends at Fulton Forest Park in Yorkshire.

So what? Your readers are interested in results and action, not funding sources or irrelevant history. Almost every story has a great bit of action that can be used to really engage the reader right up front. Whether a life change, a startling statistic or telling quote, don't be afraid to lay it on thick right from the start.

PAINT A PICTURE

Your feature may be 1,000 words long, but don't save the most interesting information until half way through. You'll have shed most of your readers by then. Use colourful and engaging writing up front, and leave the detail until later.

It's dusk, pouring with rain and 13 muddy teens slowly emerge from a narrow hole in the ground, no bigger than a dustbin lid. As each scratches their way to the surface, they turn to haul a friend from the tight tunnel they've just escaped. This is Fulton Forest Park. This is a caving weekend. And these young people have been labelled by police as some of the most troublesome in the area.

FORGET THE BIOGRAPHY

When writing up real life stories, the temptation is to give your interviewee's whole life story, before showing how your project has become involved. Starting with the change, not the back story.

The teenager steams around the corner at nearly 40mph, skids across the oily tarmac and slams the go-kart into a pile of old tyres. Time stands still for a few seconds. And then Stephen waves. Gives a thumbs up, and smiles. 'It beats stealing cars,' he shouts over the din of the others karts. 'I never went that fast in any motor I ever nicked.'

NEWS: MAIN POINTS FIRST

When reading news stories, we flick through headlines and dip into the first few lines before deciding whether to read on. So, that's where the key elements of your story need to be. Write all the main points in the first 60 words. There's no saving the best until last in news writing.

More than 300 teenagers, labelled troublesome by police, are to try climbing and canoeing on free outdoor weekends as part of a project which aims to steer them away from petty crime.

WRITE ACTIVELY

Your organisation works hard to achieve its aims, and so should your copy. Sentences like 'the overall situation was improved by the work of Save the Environment' sit passively on the page. Give your writing more pace and urgency by writing key ideas actively: 'Save the Environment improved the situation'. Remember, the cat sat on the mat. Not, the mat was sat on by the cat.

PICTURE YOUR READER

Have a picture of your target reader above your desk. Around her or him, write words or phrases to describe them. What they like doing in their spare time, what they read, what they watch on TV, what media they consume. Have that person in mind when you are writing and when you're done, review your work and ask yourself what your target person would say about it. Would they understand what you mean? Would they read to the end?

SEGMENT YOUR AUDIENCE

Don't try to talk to all of your audiences at once in a single publication, brochure, leaflet or newsletter. Most readers are only interested in content that affects them. They might miss information relevant to them because they don't bother to read past the material that isn't. Segment your audience into sizeable and sensible chunks: say volunteers, service users, funders, policy makers. For each one consider writing subtly different brochures, leaflets, or even newsletters full of well-targeted copy. If on a limited budget, ensure at least your emails and website are targeted in this way.

GET SOME SUPPORT

Identifying your audiences and their needs, ensuring your writing for them hits the mark, can be a challenge. Consider getting some charity-specific writing training, attend some writing workshops and get some critical support to improve your writing. What seems difficult at first will soon become second nature.

TAKE EVERY OPPORTUNITY

Charity publications and writing exist not just to convey information, but to get people to do something as a result of reading it. Don't miss opportunities to add boxes to the end of features and web pages asking your readers to take some action. Your brochures should have tear-off forms, your publications should carry a return postcard. Every piece of charity copy should tell your reader what to do next.

Plain English

WRITE SIMPLY

You might spend all day talking about GSPs and HWS helping your service users to engage, but that kind of language shouldn't make it into your publications.

If your reader might not easily understand what you're saying without having to read again or check another source, you need to rewrite. Resist the temptation to get all flowery and formal, just because you're writing it down. Compare:

Going forward, high-quality learning environments are an obligatory precondition for the enhancement and facilitation of the continuing learning process.

Good schools help students to learn.

JUNK THE JARGON

Every organisation has its own jargon, even if you think yours doesn't. Words and phrases you and your colleagues use every day could go over your readers' heads, no matter how clear you think you're being. Have someone not involved your organisation or work check for these blind spots, and make a list of ones to avoid.

USE ACRONYMS SPARINGLY

Spell out an acronym the first time you use it, and put the acronym in brackets: 'Not in Education, Employment or Training (NEET)'. You can use just the acronym from then on, but try not to use too many. Even if you've explained them, acronyms clog up copy and put readers off.

THE FULL STOP IS YOUR FRIEND

When there's lots of information to get across it's tempting, sometimes, to add extra bits to your sentences – like new clarifications – or fresh information – until your sentences keep running (and running) and your readers finally get lost – forget what they were meant to be reading – and then give up on your writing, because it's all become far too confusing.

It doesn't have to be this way. Break down long sentences into bite-size chunks to retain the readers' interest and keep your writing to the point. Try and allow a maximum of 30 words per sentence. If in doubt, chop a sentence into smaller parts.

TRIM THE FAT

In the best charity writing every word should pull its weight, not just fill space. To make your writing punchier, put a line through every word that doesn't earn its keep by adding to the meaning of the sentence. Look out for words like 'real', as in '*real* improvements' (as opposed to imaginary improvements?) and '*totally* unique' (something is either unique or it isn't). Most sentences can lose the word 'that' without losing any meaning.

Telling your charity's story

CREATE A JOURNEY

When you need to communicate a message, nothing works better than a brilliant story. Think about your charity's history. Who started the charity? What obstacles did they have to overcome? How successful are you now? By applying a story you can transform a list of dates into a narrative that comes alive.

INSPIRE EMPATHY

When we strongly relate with characters in a story our brains are flooded with feel-good chemicals. When writing about the people you work with, make room for simple touches that readers can relate to. Being homeless sets a little girl apart from her peers. But what makes her the same? Maybe she loves ballet, or is scared of the dark. Make the reader think: that could be me, or my daughter.

ADD A RING OF TRUTH

Adding specific details gets the reader to believe in characters. James Bond fires a Walther PPK, not just any old gun. And I bet you know his favourite cocktail too? Instead of writing 'The charity offers hot food to homeless people' try 'We give steaming cups of sweet cocoa and a welcome bowl of vegetable soup to rough sleepers who may not have eaten hot food for days'.

REMEMBER THE BIG PICTURE

Use detail in case studies and examples to remind your reader of the bigger issues at stake.

When Rasheed ran away from home he joined the 2,000 other children who go missing each year.

Try linking stories to wider events which readers may have experienced themselves. Maybe Rasheed ran away because of the rise of racist thugs in the area, or debt caused by the recession broke his family apart.

BUILD TRUST

It's all too tempting to twist a quote or manipulate a statistic to make stories a bit more powerful. But stories only retain their power if the audience trusts the storyteller. Your stories and the points you make have to be believable. Tell great stories, but make them true.

Using statistics

USE ONLY THE BEST

Choose only the most impressive numbers your charity has and use them sparingly. Research for a conservation charity found that 99% of volunteers felt more positive about themselves after being involved with a project. The research might have found much more besides, but using that striking figure by itself will have more impact than a list of findings.

The statistic that one in three of us will get cancer didn't start off that way. It began as lots of dry lists of stats that were crunched down. Get to know your material, and the best statistics will emerge.

MAKE NUMBERS EASY TO DIGEST

Make statistics accessible for your reader. '24% of people' sounds like something out of a maths equation. How about 'a quarter', 'one in four of us' or even 'one person in the average family/workplace/bus stop'? Suddenly, what seems like an irrelevant number comes a lot closer to home. Instead of saying '31% less', try 'reduced by a third'. Don't be afraid to round figures up. If your figure is 87 people out of 100, then write 'nine out of 10'.

GET YOUR READER TO VISUALISE

Rather than talking about 5,000 hectares of forest being destroyed each day, work out how many football stadiums that would be, or whether it's the same size as a particular town. Most people can't visualise one hectare, let alone 5,000.

If something is heavy, how many buses does it weigh? If something is a long distance, how many times the distance from here to Paris? How many swimming pools would it fill? How far up the Empire State Building would it reach?

PULL NUMBERS OUT

If you have lots of shocking statistics, don't clutter the main story with them. Put one or two of the most important ones in your story and explain what they mean. Then put all the other big numbers in an easy-to-read box, table or panel at the side.

KNOW YOUR SOURCES

Whether it's your own research, or someone else's, make sure you say where the statistic comes from. If you can't locate its source, or the source is not reliable, don't use it. Beware of statistics that have become common parlance in your organisation, but no-one remembers where they came from. Don't risk losing trust because you can't back up what you say.

DON'T BECOME IMMUNE

You may have become so used to hearing your own numbers that you could forget how shocking they might be for other people. Try to think from the perspective of someone who doesn't work with you – better still, ask a friend what makes their jaw drop.

GET BEHIND THE NUMBERS

Remember, your statistics are often real people or will have an impact upon them. In stories heavy with numbers, include some case studies and examples of what those statistics mean in terms of human beings and lives changed.

Using quotes

QUOTE THE IMPORTANT STUFF

Quotes are like salt and pepper. Use them sparingly to add flavour to your story. Don't add too much or you'll spoil the lot. Use quotes to highlight the most exciting and interesting things interviewees have to say. Don't put in every detail they utter, or you'll reduce the impact.

USE QUOTES TO MOVE STORIES ON

Don't use quotes to repeat information you've already given. Instead, make sure they move the story on or highlight your key messages. Your reader should get the gist of the story and your key ideas by reading the quotes alone.

DON'T BE AFRAID TO EDIT

The way people speak can look stilted and confused when written down, so it's fine to edit. Cut out words and phrases, change the order of things, add in punctuation. Just don't change the meaning. Ask your interviewee to approve your finished quotes if you're worried about misrepresenting them.

CHECK QUOTATION GRAMMAR

■ **Full stops should go inside the quote mark if you're quoting full sentences, outside if you're not.**

He said: 'It's a great move for our charity.'
The Chief Executive called it 'a great move for the charity'.

■ **If you cut a quote in half, end the first part with a comma.**

'We raised a huge amount of money,' he said. 'I'm so proud of our volunteers.'

■ **In news stories, quotes should be introduced in the past tense: she said. In features, it's more usual to use the present tense: she says.**

■ **Be consistent with your use of double or single quotation marks. There's no strict rule, so pick a style and stick to it across your organisation's publications.**

■ **Most organisations use double quotation marks when a quote appears by itself.**

"Please support our charity," he said.

■ **Most organisations use single quotes when reporting speech within another quote.**

"He said to the audience: 'please support our charity', and they did," according to the press officer.

Writing colourfully

SET THE SCENE

Descriptions of your surroundings and the people you're interviewing add life to your piece and make subtle points. A few chosen details can bring sharp images to mind and evoke sympathy for your charity or case study.

As she spoke, she plucked at the ragged seams of the grubby cardigan she wore over an ill-fitting sweater. We sat next to the damp cardboard box that had been her bed last night. A half-eaten sandwich had been tucked away for later.

DON'T GO OVERBOARD WITH COLOUR

A few, well-chosen observations will do the job.

A whiteboard outside her office announces today's business; meetings begin at 8am and she finishes the day with a magazine awards dinner at 7pm. In a homely touch, her dress for the occasion is hanging up in her spacious office.

This is enough to tell us that the interviewee is a busy, important woman, but gives the impression she's normal with it. Resist the temptation to overwrite. You're trying to get message across, not win a prize for writing.

IT ISN'T ABOUT YOU

Describe what you see, hear and smell, rather than your reaction to it. Better to get your reader to imagine how they would react to those senses. Occasionally, it might be appropriate to drop in what you're feeling, but leave 'I' out of the piece as much as possible.

DON'T USE CLICHÉS

Descriptions like the young people are 'tough nuts to crack at first' and at the end of the marathon our supporter was 'as tired as a dog' are boring and have lost their meaning. Their effect is reduced because people have read them so many times. Think of something new and more attention grabbing to say.

DON'T MIX METAPHORS

'When the volunteer made his speech at the event, he struck a spark that massaged the audience's conscience' is a mixed metaphor because 'spark' and 'massaged' don't relate to each other. 'He struck a spark that electrified the audience's conscience' is better.

Writing for marketing

TARGET YOUR WRITING

The more targeted your sales- and marketing-focused writing, the more effective it will be. Think of the ideal reader and why they would take the action you want them to take. What are their interests and motivations? What is the 'pain' that they have, that your product or service can solve? Write about the problem and your solution, in the language that your target audience uses. For each different target audience, write subtly different copy addressing their particular needs. Make the reader feel you're talking directly to them.

SELL BENEFITS, NOT FEATURES

Emphasise the benefits (the outcomes) of your service ahead of its features (what it does). Writing about what the reader will gain from your services or product is much more powerful than describing what they are. So, instead of 'You'll be able to speak to one of our advisers', try 'Our advisers can tell you about hundreds of jobs in your area'.

UPSKILL YOURSELF

Copywriting, or writing for marketing that gets people to do things, is a very specific skill and takes lots of practice. There are things that work time and again, and techniques you can learn that always seem to generate results. Get some professional training on writing for marketing, and never stop learning how to improve.

OFFER SOMETHING USEFUL

People are bombarded with advertising all day, every day. Give them an incentive to open your brochure or web page by offering something useful, like a PDF of practical tips or a free booklet. Think about what knowledge you can share that will be of value to your reader, and offer it to them in exchange for their attention – or better still, their contact details.

ADDRESS YOUR READER

Make it clear who you are writing for from the start so your reader doesn't lose interest:

Does your local authority need help to get young people into work in your area? Our new service could help you.

Address your reader directly using the word 'you' to help build rapport. For example, when you're writing for service users, 'we can help you find a job' is more engaging than 'we help young unemployed people find work'. Tell the reader what it has to do with them.

USE BUZZ WORDS

John, Now, Free, Proof, Important and Easy are the most effective words you can use to sell your services.

Addressing your reader by name ('John') in your writing means they are more likely to read on as they'll think you're writing to them personally. The words 'now' and 'important' give your writing urgency:

It's important that you sign up now.

Everyone wants something for 'free'. If it's 'easy' it means it saves your reader valuable time. 'Proof' will give your pitch a sense of legitimacy:

We have a proven track record of finding people jobs.

Writing a speech

MAKE A PLAN

Before you start writing any speech, jot down some ideas on who your audience is and what you aim to make them do, feel and think. Note the three or four key messages you want to get across. Everything you write should appeal to this audience and contribute to conveying your key messages. Consider inventing a person who represents the majority of your audience and write as if you're speaking directly to them.

LOOK FOR A NEW ANGLE

Think about what you can include to make your presentation innovative and engaging. 'Five things you didn't know about Save the Animals' work in the UK' will intrigue your audience more than 'About Save the Animals'. Try to include stories, painting pictures of lives changed or people in need. Consider linking what you're saying to something topical in the news, making your presentation relevant and up-to-date.

INCLUDE JOKES AND ANECDOTES

Use jokes and anecdotes to add warmth to your speech and help your audience relate to you. Anecdotes offer your audience an understanding of, and empathy for, your story that statistics and facts might not achieve.

But think carefully about which jokes and anecdotes will work, and how many are appropriate for your audience. An audience of young people might like a lot of jokes but a board of trustees is less likely to want a laugh a minute. Don't be afraid to push at the limits, to make your speech stand out.

CRAFT YOUR WORDS

Once you've written down the basics, edit to give your speech more power and excite your audience. Short sentences have more impact than long ones and make it less likely you'll fluff your words. Repeat key phrases to build emphasis and drama. Martin Luther King repeated 'I have a dream' 11 times during his famous 1963 speech.

Talk to your audience directly, asking for action: 'Get involved' and 'Help us achieve our vision'. Rhetorical questions are a good way of introducing a new section of your presentation: 'What are the problems facing young people today?'

MAKE A POINT, TELL A STORY

Reinforce what you're saying by first making a point and then telling a story or giving an example.

We urgently need to help homeless teenagers in London. Let me tell you about Richard. He's been on the streets for a year.

Sum up by bringing all the strands together, explaining why they support your key point. Give your audience something to take home and think about.

Writing for young people

BREAK UP YOUR COPY

Be creative with how you present information. Reams of continuous writing isn't going to get young people interested in protecting dolphins. Instead, include chunks of information presented in various ways.

Consider including a quiz about whether a dolphin is more intelligent than 10 other animals; a download: The Top Five Things You Never Knew About Dolphins; a picture story: Seven Famous Dolphins; and maybe a fact-sheet: All You Need to Know About How a Dolphin's Brain Works.

DITCH THE SLANG

It's, like, totally sic that you are down with the kidz but regurgitating the Urban Dictionary in your charity copy isn't going to impress your youth audience. It sounds forced and patronising. Instead, adopt a plain English tone and explain key terms simply. Don't try to use slang or misplaced humour.

Cyber bullying is when someone uses the internet or texts to repeatedly harass, harm or hurt another person.

ONE IDEA AT A TIME

Young people are used to receiving information in bite-size chunks; that's why Tweets and texts are so popular. Don't overload your copy with too many key messages. Think about the one action you want young readers to take, and concentrate on that.

Say you want to get young people to call your drugs and alcohol helpline: tell them why they might call and how that call will help make life better. You may also run a drop-in centre, a homework group or short breaks for teenagers, but don't mention these. Tell them about those once they've called.

TALK TO THEM

Your charity listens to children and young people, right? Talk to them about how they like to be communicated with. Talk to young people you know, whether your kids, the teenager next door or young volunteers in your organisation. Ask them what they like and dislike, what they think of your issue and what their concerns are. Note down the actual words they use, and then reproduce them in your writing. Even better, get them to look over your writing or have a go themselves.

Beating writers' block

GET COMFORTABLE

It's no use trying to write somewhere you feel uncomfortable or where you're going to be constantly interrupted by colleagues. Escape your desk and find a quieter corner of the office. Or you could work at home. If you prefer a bit of background noise, work in a cafe. Music, rather than radio talk shows, can help the words flow.

GET INSPIRED

Look at some publications or articles similar to the one you're trying to write. If you're writing for your charity's newsletter, visit other charities' websites and see what theirs look like; it might spark a great idea. Challenge yourself to copy the style of a particular piece, but don't plagiarise.

START WITH A STRUCTURE

If you're unsure what angle your piece should take, write a series of headlines or titles to give yourself some direction. Don't waste time seeking out that pithy quote or striking statistic. Think big picture rather than detail at this stage. Come back and refine later.

START IN THE MIDDLE

Starting a piece can be a little daunting; it's easy to get bogged down in making the introduction just perfect. If you don't know where to begin, move on and start with another section of the piece. Just getting some words down on the page as quickly as possible or doing a 'brain dump' will make you feel like you're getting somewhere.

DON'T ALLOW INTERRUPTIONS

Turn off your telephone. Turn off your email. Ask colleagues not to disturb you. Give yourself an hour just to get started without interruptions. You'll get so bored you'll start writing just for something to do.

BREAK YOUR TASK UP

It can be overwhelming if you're writing something like your annual review that's going to take days or weeks, and must be of the highest quality. Break your task into smaller chunks and set deadlines for each part. Writing will become much less intimidating and will give you a sense of satisfaction each time you complete a section.

HAVE A BREAK

Writing requires a high level of concentration that you can only sustain for so long – no more than a couple of hours. Take regular, proper breaks and that doesn't mean checking your emails. Go for a walk, make a cup of tea, stretch, have a chat with a colleague. But be strict and go back to your writing after 15 minutes.

Charity publications

The publications process

START WITH A PLAN

Your communications team may have the charity sector's best writers and designers. But without rigorous editorial processes, all that talent can pull in different directions. That could mean a project ends up being delivered way past deadline and over budget.

A solid editorial plan, mapping your project from beginning to end, will ensure everyone knows what's expected of them, who's in charge of what, and in what time frame they have to do their part.

CREATE A CLEAR BRIEF

Every writing project should have clear objectives. Ask yourself: who is the audience? What is the budget? What is the timeframe? What do we want readers to do? How will the document be used? By whom? What are the project's success factors? What are the risks? Put all this information into a single document that is circulated to everyone involved in your publication, including external suppliers. Ensure everyone understands it and those who need to sign it off have done so before the project begins.

ORGANISE A TIMETABLE

Break the project down into easily manageable steps: writing first and second drafts, briefing designers, design and layout, iterative tweaks to the copy and design, proofreading and sending to print. Set a deadline for each part and outline who is responsible for carrying out each aspect of the work. Build in just enough flexibility to deal with unexpected events and problems.

NARROW THE LOOP

If you're working on an important project, it's likely that lots of people in your charity will want to have a say. That's fine, but let them give their opinions once, and at the right time. For example, your first draft might go out to everyone from volunteers to your Chief Executive for their views.

But as you move on to second and third drafts, the pool of people giving their opinions should get smaller and smaller. Final sign-off for print should be just one or two people. If everyone is allowed to butt in at every stage, you'll constantly be making amendments and never get anything done.

BORROW ANOTHER PAIR OF EYES

Before any work goes off to senior staff, make sure someone else (preferably someone who is not involved with the project) looks over your publication to check for problems. Once you've worked with copy for a while it takes a fresh pair of eyes to point out errors you've missed, and to offer constructive feedback. Before copy is finally sent to the printers, be sure to use professional proofreaders to sort out any lingering typos. Proofreading is the last thing you should do before print. Make sure everyone has made all the changes they want before beginning the proofing process.

DON'T GET TOO ATTACHED

It's easy to become attached to your work when you've sweated over it. But that's exactly when you should let go. Approach criticism and editing as a vital part of the creative process. The only way to improve your writing is to have others read over it and make suggestions. Consider joining a writing mentoring group.

EVALUATE YOUR PROCESS

Once you've hit the 'print' button, make time for a thorough evaluation of the process – not just the finished product. What worked well and which parts could have gone more smoothly? Invite feedback from those involved and gather their valuable insights into the process. Don't forget to keep a note of them, and ensure constructive suggestions are incorporated next time.

Style guides

CREATE A SIMPLE STYLE GUIDE

Do you write 'the government' or 'the Government'? Is it 'our charity is' or 'our charity are'? Coordinate or co-ordinate? Ten per cent or 10%? Make sure everyone follows an agreed style guide to raise the standard of your charity's written communications. It also makes life easier for new staff, as well as external writers and proofers, to get up to speed with how your charity writes. Create a simple guide for your charity now, keep it in a central place and keep adding to it as you make more decisions about style. (Use some of the following tips for inspiration.)

DECIDE WHO YOU ARE

There's often room for confusion in something as simple as your charity's name. Do you refer to yourself as a charity, an organisation, a not for profit, or something else? What is the charity's strapline and when should it be used? Is your name spelled out in full or do you ever use an abbreviation? How do you describe your charity in five words? In a line? In a paragraph? Get your decisions down on paper, then circulate to ensure everyone uses them consistently.

CLARIFY YOUR CAPITALS

Many people in the Charity Sector like to use Capitals whenever referring to An Important Thing in their Organisation. A publication like *The Guardian*, by contrast, uses lower case for practically everything except proper names. Your communications are likely to include lots of job titles, names of projects, and names of organisations. Too many capitals slow up your copy and make it stilted, but too few and you'll have the grammar police writing in. Add a few basic rules to your style guide, then stick to them.

DEFINE USE OF NUMBERS

Do you write US$10m, $10,000,000 or ten million dollars? Is it 10km or 10 k.m. – or just over six miles? Percent, per cent or %? Charity reports are often full of figures, which is confusing enough. Don't make it worse by flipping between different ways of presenting them.

IDENTIFY SENSITIVE PHRASES

You won't find young people's charities talking about 'the youth of today' or HIV charities referring to 'AIDS victims'. Choose the right wording to describe people and things to present a strong and united voice, and to ensure new staff, volunteers and external suppliers don't use phrases that aren't on-message. Without pandering to oversensitivity or political correctness, put together some common-sense guidelines and add to your style guide.

FIND YOUR CLICHÉS

As well as your own jargon, your charity will have a few stock phrases you use time and again because they have a good ring to them, or it's easier to use them than write something new. Make sure you don't bore your audience, or worse, turn them off completely, by writing the same thing in the same way, time and again.

Layout

USE POWERFUL PICTURES

A photograph of four charity executives wearing suits next to the charity logo and a cheque won't draw a reader in. A photo of them abseiling down a city skyscraper in fancy dress certainly would. Always choose the most active and striking image you can. When taking or commissioning photos, go for interesting angles, ask your subject to do something active (rather than just stand there), or think of a novel way to present a boring subject.

USE HIGH-RESOLUTION IMAGES

Always take and use the highest quality photo that you can. Most digital cameras have different resolution settings, so ensure yours is set to the largest one. To be of print quality, an image needs to be at least 2MB in size. As a rule of thumb, it should fill your computer screen and still look perfectly defined. Don't stretch or 'blow up' a small image to fit a space, as it will print blurred and pixelated. If in doubt, choose another image.

GOOD PICTURE CAPTIONS

If readers are intrigued by the picture, chances are they'll read what's written underneath. Use that to get your messages across. Don't just list who's in the picture:

From left to right: John Jones, Jane Smith and Jack Evans pictured at last Thursday's meeting.

Instead, fill your caption with information that engages your reader, and moves the story on. Remember, it might be the only thing they read.

The sky's the limit: supporters of Our Charity abseiled 1,000 feet to raise money to help Tanzanian children go to school.

USE PULL QUOTES

Choose a powerful sentence or phrase from your article, and have your designer make it into a 'pull quote' by printing it large in the middle of the text. As well as making the page easier to read by breaking it into manageable chunks, pull quotes give you the opportunity to hammer home key messages. Choose something powerful, shocking, or emotional, but don't overuse. One or two are enough.

CREATE BOX OUTS

Instead of presenting what you have to say in one large block of text, separate out lists, case studies, long quotes or calls to action into boxes. These 'box outs' can give readers easily digestible information at a glance. Don't be tempted to put everything in a box. More than a couple in your article will make things crowded, and your reader won't know where to start. Box outs should be short and to the point, without preamble or fluff.

TIDY UP WEB LINKS

Links to websites are a pain to put into print. They can be long, impossible to cut and can create irritating layout problems when inserted into your article. Instead, create a box out of links at the bottom of the page so your reader can use them when they've finished reading.

DON'T NEGLECT PAGE FURNITURE

Page numbers, issue dates, page headings and footers may add to your publication if you get them right. But get them wrong, and they throw the credibility of your publication out of kilter. Eagle eyed readers can't help but pay more attention to non-consecutive page numbers or misspelled titles than to what you're trying to say. Don't give them the pleasure. Check this 'page furniture' as closely as the rest of the text, if not closer.

Online writing

Writing for the web

KEEP IT BRIEF

It is difficult to read from a screen. Keep everything short to avoid losing readers' attention. Sentences should be no longer than a line, and never more than 30 words. Keep paragraphs under three lines, subheads three or four words, and web pages fewer than 400 words overall. You should always create more pages rather than making your reader scroll.

OFFER ACTIONS

Each page should have a purpose, so offer your readers an action to carry out, or links to other parts of the site. Browsers are used to being told what to do, so do point them in the direction you want them to go. Do you want people to find out more about a specific area of your work? To donate? Sign a petition? Visit another section of your website? Think about the action your page might lead to before you even start writing.

TARGET MULTIPLE AUDIENCES

The web allows you to talk to lots of different audiences without much additional investment. Think about who your different readers are likely to be (or you would like them to be) and split up your site into different sections. If you can, write the same copy in three slightly different ways targeted at your three different audiences. Don't force browsers to navigate through content that's irrelevant to them in order to find content that is. They won't bother.

WRITE FOR SCANNERS

People don't read web pages: they scan them. Make it easy for impatient visitors to pick up your key messages. Use lists and bullets. Put important points in bold. Break up your writing with subheads. Use devices like boxes and colours to draw focus, but make sure the page doesn't become too cluttered. Blank space gives the eyes a rest.

BE CONSISTENT

Charities frequently allow lots of people in the organisation to upload their own content. That's great, but do ensure contributors write in a consistent, compelling way, observing basic web writing tips. This is where your style guide becomes particularly important. Distribute a copy to anyone who is able to update your site.

PICK THE RIGHT KEYWORDS

Keywords and keyphrases are the words that people put into a search engine when they're trying to locate something on the web. For instance, people might end up at a cancer charity's website by typing in 'cancer treatment' or 'chemotherapy'. They help web browsers find content that's relevant to them. If you want them to find you, fill your web pages with the keywords and phrases those most interested in what you do or offer are likely to type into a search engine.

AVOID GIBBERISH

In the early days of search engine technology, web writers would simply stuff their copy full of keywords to the point where it stopped making sense. Even today you still see copy like:

Charity, the charity sector, charity supporters and charity professionals are what our leading charity is all about.

Search engines are savvier now and will screen out such blatant attempts to trick them. As a rule, your keyword should appear in less than 7% of your copy. But search engines change all the time. Get some up-to-date training on writing for the web, as well as support to identify relevant but low competition keywords, if you want to get to the top of search engine results.

MAKE HEADINGS WORK

However clever or full of puns your headlines are, they will not work online. And they won't help search engines send people to your site. Headlines are the most important part of your web writing, so don't waste them. Make them simple, clear and descriptive of the copy that follows them. Ensure you include some keywords that web browsers are looking for. Remember, your headline is most likely to be what appears in search engine results.

UPDATE COPY REGULARLY

Viewers expect sites to be updated at least once a week – many times a day for news sites. Search engines reward sites which update content regularly with higher rankings. So write short and often for your website. If putting together a long story or article, can you drip it out over two or three days, instead of posting in one go? Create a reason for visitors to come back to your site again and again.

Writing for Twitter

PRIORITISE AND FOCUS

Pick one key message. Your newsletter might be about five or six things, but if you try to say it all, you'll lose all impact:

Discounts in our shop, new fairtrade suppliers, prizes and free gifts.

Concentrate on stopping readers in their tracks, not bombarding them with information. Once they've clicked on your link, that's when they're ready to absorb more.

Your free fairtrade gift is waiting.

USE WORDS THAT WORK

People like to read about themselves and hear personal stories. Words like 'you', 'your' and 'my' will work well in short, sharp phrases.

Your guide to saving money.

How the Foundation saved my life.

Use a number to give instant impact.

10 things you didn't know about our planet.

We all love a top tip – especially if it means something will be easy, quick or save us money. So use sentences that start with 'How to'.

How to save energy in your home.

ASK QUESTIONS

Asking a question is one of the strongest ways to engage people using just a few words. They immediately get attention because they demand an answer from the reader. Questions also help you ensure you're addressing the right audience. Those who click on your Tweet are those most likely to be receptive to the messaging behind the question you're asking.

Are you drinking too much?

Do you care for a loved one?

Are you job hunting?

CUT THE FLUFF

Put your most important words right at the front of your Tweets – don't save the best until last and cut out any words that don't add to what you're saying. This will help readers instantly understand what the Tweet is about. Instead of:

New report shows there are over 2 million people affected by floods in Pakistan.

We need people to help us by running the London marathon.

Try:

2 million people hit by Pakistan floods.

Run the marathon, help disabled children.

BE CLEAR

Don't abbreviate everything or opt for acronyms to save space. You may cram more in, but your message will be harder to understand.

HL conf, 5Mar11: 20 tkts left. Save ££ & see Gov't spkrs.

Instead, concentrate on one clear message that will get your reader to engage, click and read on. Avoid too many capital letters or non-essential punctuation.

Housing chief will 'justify sector cuts' at conference.

Writing news and features

News writing

GET TO THE POINT

When writing news stories, don't give the background before you've told the reader what the main point of the story is. Your reader doesn't care about reports, how research was carried out, where funding came from or even who did it until they know what the actual news is you're trying to share.

The Sea Welfare Group has published extensive research into whether fish feel pain, after three years of studies by academics at the University of Portsmouth. The research, which received over £1 million of funding from the European Animal Welfare Council, looked at dozens of species of fish, squid and other sea creatures by collecting them and measuring their trauma under different conditions. Researchers found many species of fish experienced 'serious trauma' from all kinds of fishing, including hook-and-line and trawler fishing...

Where's the story? At best, it's the end of the third sentence. Don't make your reader wait that long, because they won't.

Fish experience 'serious trauma' from all kinds of fishing, according to a new study.

USE THE NEWS PYRAMID

Think of a pyramid, with the 'point' of your story right at the top. You only have a very narrow amount of space at the top of the pyramid, so your writing there should be short and sharp. Never more than 30 words. Use slightly more words to write the second bit of information, and like a pyramid it should 'prop up' the bit above it, expanding and explaining it.

Tuna fish feel pain even when caught with a hook and line, researchers have found. The study revealed sea fish are less traumatised by rod fishing than being caught in a trawler's net, but that they still suffered distress.

USE A QUOTE EARLY

Use a quote from an expert in the first three sentences, and ensure it moves the story on rather than simply restating it.

Simon Smith, head of marine biology at The Sea Welfare Group, said: 'These findings should raise questions about what has previously been regarded as ethical fishing.'

WRITE FOR THE READER

How you approach a news story should depend on who it is written for. Think not of the story, but its effect on the reader. The reader wants to know: what has this got to do with me? Consider the angle to take for a publication aimed at fishermen:

The fishing industry could face even tougher restrictions on its methods, after researchers found line fishing causes extreme trauma in tuna.

Compare it with the same story, aimed at environmentalists:

Green shoppers are questioning whether eating line-caught fish is as ethical as they thought, following publication of new research.

USE IDENTIFIABLE EXAMPLES

Your reader will be looking for something familiar to identify with. Pick a celebrity, or an everyday object or occurrence your reader can quickly recognise, and talk about your story's effect on them.

Ethical celebrity chef Jamie Oliver was dealt a blow last night after it emerged that one of his favourite ingredients, fresh fish, does feel pain when caught on a hook and line.

Hungry Brits could face paying an extra £1.50 for a bag of fish and chips, as fishermen respond to new restrictions on trawler fishing for cod.

EIGHT WAYS TO STRUCTURE A FEATURE

■ **TRADITIONAL**
Give a topical introduction and present different angles to the story with some quotes and case studies illustrating them. Add some observations, draw some conclusions and sum up.

■ **FIRST PERSON**
Write from your own point of view, about an experience you've been through or an activity you've tried. This approach can bring real authenticity and life to a piece. 'The day I...'

■ **CASE STUDY**
Write a piece centred around a single case study. You can still include extra information on the issue here and there, but let the interviewee's story highlight the main points. Consider writing the piece completely in the first person from the interviewee's point of view, like a letter or diary entry.

■ **QUESTION AND ANSWER**
Draw up a list of questions about your topic that your reader might want an answer to and set about composing responses. Include quotes and extra information, or perhaps get experts to answer the questions for you. A really clear and concise way to give information on a particular topic.

■ **TOP TIPS AND LISTS**
10 things you didn't know about... Five tips for... The year's 20 best... Writing your issue in short lists are a creative way to convey information. They're easy to write, easy to read and you can make them as serious or lightweight as the subject demands.

■ **A-Z**
Make a list of pieces of information, each beginning with a different letter of the alphabet for a fun, easy-to-read way of conveying ideas to your reader. The A-Z is particularly good if you have writer's block, and don't know where to start.

■ **PHOTO STORY**
A picture can be worth a thousand words, so they say. Even more if you write a fantastic picture caption or short text to accompany the image. Use photographs to tell your story, with some telling words to hammer your message home.

■ **DEAR DEIDRE**
A problem page format can be fun and engaging. Think of questions your reader might like answered and draw up agony aunt responses. Serious and humorous tones work equally well.

Starting your features

FIND A TOPICAL REFERENCE

Introduce your feature with a 'hot' issue of the day. Something everyone is talking about and how it might be affecting your readers. Once you've got their attention, link your hot issue to what you need to say and proceed from there. But beware, hot topics go out of date very quickly so might not be suitable for publications that take months to get to print.

GENERATE SOME MYSTERY

Sam Pringle is a man on a mission. Tasked with running 13 half marathons in 13 months, he's become a slave to the treadmill and sees more of his physiotherapist than he does his girlfriend.

This introduction poses more questions than it answers. It intrigues the reader so they want to find out more. Use the most unique, unexpected angle of your story to draw readers in. The best features set up a tease, then drip-feed answers throughout the piece to keep the reader engaged.

TALK DIRECTLY TO THE READER

Do you give to charity? Do you ever wonder what happens to your money before it's put to use? Charity donors will be relieved to know that over half of UK charities have an ethical investment policy.

The direct appeal is a quick win. Ideal for potentially dry or complicated features, it gets your reader to do some of the work by questioning themselves.

BECOME A FLY ON THE WALL

An eyewitness account places the reader in the midst of the action and they'll read on to find out what happens. Set up the main issues by telling the colourful story of someone involved. Remember to revisit the action throughout your feature, to add a change of pace and create a satisfying feeling of completion when the feature ends.

Being pushed from side to side, Mary struggles to hold up her placard urging an end to global poverty. She can hardly see above the shoving crowd or keep up with chants about a hundred different issues. Her own message drowned out, she wonders if it's worth being here at all.

CAPTIVATE WITH A QUOTE

"I didn't feel it was possible to achieve much in a career. I never felt I fitted into society. I didn't go out much because I didn't feel comfortable around people. I was scared people would find out about my disability."

Starting your feature with a hard-hitting quote will pull readers in. The reader is likely to read on because they empathise and engage with the person speaking.

BREAK FROM THE NORM

Disabled people can't contribute as much as others.

Beginning a feature with a controversial statement is a sure-fire way to attract your reader's eye, following it up with an explanation of course. Push at the edges of your readers' comfort zone to get them interested in what you have to say.

Writing press releases

ASK YOURSELF IF IT'S REALLY NEWS

Before you start writing your press release, stop and think: is this piece of information really worth a press release? Is it strong enough to make it into the media? Have you actually got something new to say, or are you just recycling old news? When your press release hits journalists' inboxes, those are the first questions they'll be asking. Send journalists a steady stream of weak, irrelevant stories and they'll stop even opening your emails.

TAILOR YOUR MESSAGE

Centre your press release on what your story has to do with the target audience of the publication or media outlet you're targeting. How will it make the reader mad, glad or sad? People don't care about your story until they know what it has to do with them.

If you were opening a youth drop-in centre, your press release for the local youth website might read:

Guitar lessons, pool competitions and a graffiti art wall – they're all on offer at a new centre for 15-18 year olds in Salford.

But if you were targeting a community paper, read by local residents, you would position your press release differently:

The streets may feel safer in Salford, thanks to new drop-in centre for young people. The centre aims to tackle the boredom that can lead to petty crime.

MAKE YOUR SUBJECT LINE SING

A good subject line is the difference between a journalist opening your emailed press release and hitting the delete key. Spend time crafting the email subject line to make it attention-grabbing. 'Half of older people feel isolated' is a better subject line than 'Press release: new report'.

GET TO THE POINT

Writing a good press release is the same as writing good news. Start with the most exciting angle you have to grab journalists' attention. Always keep in mind that journalists (and everyone else) are most interested in the results of what you do, not how those results came about.

A third more women could survive breast cancer with better treatment, a study has shown.

Is better than:

A recent study was carried out into breast cancer treatment. 5,982 women were surveyed and asked how long it took to get treatment...

GET THE BASICS RIGHT

Language should be clear, concise, active and jargon-free. Sentences should be fewer than 30 words and the whole press release should take no more than one side of A4. Bear in mind that most journalists are overworked. Sending them a well-written press release that they only have to change slightly will often give your story a better chance of making publication.

HAVE GOOD QUOTES

Journalists expect quotes to be included in your release, so get them in as early as you can. Quotes show you have someone journalists can speak to, and that you understand their needs. Sometimes your quote may be the only part of your release they use, so inject some passion and controversy into them, and ensure the main points you need to make are included.

OFFER CASE STUDIES

There's nothing a journalist loves more than human interest. How is the issue in your press release affecting people? Do you have an example to share? You must have some case studies ready and be willing to speak to the press the day your release goes out. No case studies often mean no chance of publication.

Charity annual reports

SEE THEM AS AN OPPORTUNITY

It may have to include your charity's accounts but there's no excuse for your annual report to be a dull document full of figures. There's plenty of room for case studies, great storytelling and images that make an impact. Do it well and your annual report is the perfect showcase and marketing tool. Since you have to publish one anyway, you might as well make it work for your organisation.

STATE THE OBVIOUS

Many annual reports fail to explain what the charity actually does, and why. Make sure you include this in the first couple of pages. Don't expect readers to understand automatically why your charity's activities are important. You need to explain who you've helped and exactly what difference it has made to their lives. Use your annual report to bust any misconceptions about your organisation, and address any concerns donors have.

MAKE SURE YOU SHINE

Your charity's achievements are not just awards won, or large donations received. Think about anything that has furthered your aims and objectives. How much press coverage did your new service or report receive? Have you made recommendations that have influenced government policy? Have you won new contracts or recruited new members?

MEET THE REQUIREMENTS

The Charity Commission, the Office of the Scottish Charity Regulator and the Charity Commission for Northern Ireland all publish detailed guidance on what information your annual report must include. Use that as a starting point, but build upon it to create a story rather than simply reporting back. In particular, pay attention to how you demonstrate the impact your charity has had on its service users and the wider public.

CONSIDER HOW REPORTS ARE READ

However hard you work on your annual report, assume most people will read only headlines, picture captions, box outs and the occasional pull quote. Ensure these elements offer the key messages you need to get across, without the reader having to delve deeper. Highlight any particular calls to action or appeals for support. Don't bury them in the text.

TALK ABOUT YOUR PROBLEMS

It's easy to paint a picture of what's gone well, but what about when things haven't gone to plan? Showing how you've overcome challenges might be a powerful way to cement support. It shows an honesty readers can relate to, generating further sympathy for the cause.

LOOK TO THE FUTURE

Where possible show how this year's achievements fit in to your longer-term goals. Explain what still needs to be done, recognise any challenges you face, and how you're going to manage any risk involved. Offer your readers the big picture, not just snippets of the year gone by. Help them to understand your charity is both effective in the short term, but also has a strategic direction.

TELL PEOPLE HOW THEY CAN HELP...

...and how you can help them. Your report will have inspired people, so make sure they know what to do next. Don't just present information and expect your reader to decide what to do about it. Offer clear and concrete actions for readers to do before they put your report down. Direct them to your website, have a donation form, or ask them to tear off a postcard and return it. You reader should never have to ask: what should I do now?

DEMONSTRATE YOUR IMPACT

Tell the story of the difference your organisation makes, not just what you do. Think of the concrete outcomes behind your statistics, behind the nuts and bolts of how you actually deliver the service. Think about wider impacts as well as direct ones. Your meals on wheels service may help older people to have a hot meal each day, but it also reduces their isolation, lessens the chance of a trip or fall, meaning health services save money. Try to describe the 'long tail' of your activity, and back it up with evidence.

COLLECT DATA YOU CAN REPORT

Effective impact reporting isn't just about the difference that you think you make. Ask those who receive your service what they get out of it. What can they do now they otherwise couldn't? Can you find a way to measure it? Do they feel happier now than before? More self-confident? Good impact reporting requires a long-term investment in finding out how lives might be changed by your service, then continually measuring how they really are changed as the project progresses.

EXPLORE THE UNEXPECTED

You may be surprised that a service is making a difference to people's lives in a way your charity never expected or intended. A helpline that few people call might be considered a failure and cancelled. But what if potential users of the helpline are less worried about an issue simply because they know the helpline is there if they need it? Your annual report is an ideal place to tell more complex stories that a brochure or leaflet might not allow. If you show a huge and wide-ranging impact, with just low-level intervention, you can show funders their money is being made to work incredibly hard.

Writing case studies

WRITE ABOUT CHANGE

When writing case studies make sure change is central to the story. What was your case study doing before you got involved, what did you do, and what are they like now? What do they think their life would be like if you hadn't intervened? Supporters want to read about outcomes and impact, so ensure your case studies show it.

I didn't leave the house for 10 years and felt uncomfortable around people I didn't know. Now I'm a different person.

If there wasn't a place like this, Stacey would still be hanging around on the street, smoking and drinking. Instead she's going to college each day.

SHOW, DON'T TELL

Instead of stating your arguments, allow the stories of the people you work with to make the case for you. You're bound to say you need money and that your issue is of vital importance. Write your case studies in such a way that readers come to those conclusions for themselves, giving them extra weight and credibility. Engage your audience by involving them in the experience, not hammering them with polemic. Once you've built the case through the story itself, ask for the action.

USE A POWERFUL OPENING

You have seconds to attract a reader's attention, so don't waste it by filling the start of your case study with background information. Try to make the introduction either striking or surprising, or consider using an opening that is a little intriguing, without being so mysterious your reader won't engage or will miss the point.

I realised I had two alternatives facing me: prison or death.

Paula moved to the countryside with her husband in her early 20s, went shopping for a table and came home with a goat.

GET DETAILED

The more detail you can add to your case studies, the more compelling and believable they will be. Replace generalizations like 'Sam enjoyed going to school' with specifics. Little throwaway details make the case study seem more real.

Sam loved maths lessons, particularly a double session with algebraic equations.

USE REAL VOICES

Make sure your real people sound real. Show they have traits and habits that your readers and potential supporters might share. Are they a mother, are they at risk of losing their job, do they worry about money, do they get lonely? You want your reader to think 'that person could be me'. Let people's personalities come through, while tightening up their words and making it all easier to read.

KEEP THE STORY MOVING

Your case study won't say everything you need to say. Tell the story through their eyes and in their words, but use your words to fill gaps and move things along.

"I knew my life needed to change when I became a Dad," says Simon. "But I had no idea how to change."

Our support workers help 500 former prisoners like Simon every year. They offer practical help with day-to-day tasks such as job applications, shopping, benefits.

"My support worker showed me I could do stuff I never thought I could do. I've been out of prison for a year now and there's no way I'm going back."

INTERVIEWING CASE STUDIES

■ Do some preparation before you interview someone. Be sure you know what information you hope to get from the interviewee. Check that the person you want to interview is able to provide you with the information you need. Interviewees always complain about the interviewer who hasn't done his or her research.

■ Ensure that your pen works and that you have enough paper. Check the batteries in your sound recorder, if using one, and don't forget to ask permission to record. If you are travelling to meet your interviewee allow yourself plenty of time to get there.

■ Be clear with the interviewee what it is that you want to talk to them about and try to put them at ease.

■ Ensure that you are not the one doing all the talking. Listening is key. It's very frustrating for an interviewee when they're asked a question to which they've already provided the answer.

■ Don't be afraid to deviate from your planned questions if the conversation takes you on a different course, as long as the information is useful. But do steer the interviewee back to what you were discussing before they went off on a tangent.

■ If you are not getting the information you need, try to rephrase the question and leave a gap for silence after the question has been put.

Proofreading

PROOF IN THE RIGHT PLACE

Proofreading should be the very last thing done to your copy, after everyone else is happy with it. That means after the designer has laid it out, after your colleagues have made their edits, after your boss has said they're satisfied. While it's a good idea to get the copy as flawless as possible before it goes into design, a proper proofread should only take place at this very final stage.

DON'T PROOF YOUR OWN WORK

The person or people who wrote the publication should never proofread it. Writers get so used to their own copy that it's near impossible to spot mistakes. Instead, recruit someone who has never read the copy before, has not been involved in the publication and does not have a stake in it. They should be reading for errors only, not offering their opinion on your writing, style, structure or purpose.

DO A DOUBLE PROOFREAD

Your publication should be proofread twice, by two completely different proofreaders. Your first proofer makes their comments and then the changes are made. The second proofreader then does their proof. Even the best proofreaders can make mistakes and miss things. Only a double proofread can flush out all errors.

CHECK DESIGNER'S CHANGES

Check that all changes you ask for as a result of proofreading have been made properly by your designer. Designers can misunderstand what you want changed, or even introduce new errors into the copy as they correct old ones. Check too they haven't knocked boxes out of line or that their corrections haven't created single words on lines by themselves (known as 'widows') further down the copy.

TAKE A COURSE

Most people think anyone can dash off a proofread, but knowing what to look for and developing that eagle eye is a skill that needs to be learned, practiced and perfected. A proper proofreading course will give you tools, skills and confidence to do it well.

GET IN THE RIGHT MINDFRAME

Proofreading requires a high level of concentration. That means finding somewhere quiet to do it. Proofread when fresh, not in a rush at the end of the day. Always print out whatever you're proofreading, and use a ruler to guide yourself down the page. Don't attempt to proofread on screen.

LOOK FOR COMMON MISTAKES

At the proofreading stage, you shouldn't be looking to make major changes to your publication. Your 'error checklist' should include: spelling, grammar, typing errors and consistency (Are you using double or single quotation marks? Are all lists in the same format? Are the headings all the same size? Are you spelling out numbers or using numerals?). You may need to change the odd badly-worded sentence, although most of these should have been fixed by now. Look out for widows and long words being split over two lines in an ugly way.

AND NOT SO OBVIOUS ERRORS

Are the page numbers correct? Are the page numbers on the contents page correct? Are all phone numbers, addresses, email and website addresses right? Are all captions and headlines correct? Has that changed publication title been reflected throughout the document? Have footnotes been knocked onto the wrong page? Are images of sufficient resolution?

USE PROOFREADING MARKS

There is a reasonably standard set of proofreading marks that show the changes you want made in a consistent way. Use them to make what you want clear to your designer and colleagues. Search for proofreaders' marks on the internet and provide a copy of the set you are using to your designer.

FIVE CHARACTERISTICS OF A GREAT CHARITY WRITER:

A GREAT CHARITY WRITER:

1. **Reads, reads, reads...**

   Learn from the great novelists, writers and advertising copywriters, as well as the writers in the charity publications you most admire.

2. **Is always learning how to improve their craft.**

   Take training courses, buy books and toolkits. Make it your mission to keep learning about good writing and put what you learn to work.

3. **Knows they can't do it alone.**

   Get some writing mentoring, hook up with a writers' group, have others critique your work. Welcome criticism without pride, and learn from what others have to say.

4. **Gets into good habits.**

   Embrace opportunities to find out what makes you a better writer. What gets you excited to write? Where do you produce your best work? When do you find it flows better? Pin down your good writing environment, then make it a habit.

5. **Writes, writes, writes...**

   Daily. All kinds of formats. All kinds of styles. All the time. The more you exercise your writing muscle, particularly in the company of other writers, the better your writing will become.

"I'm amazed at the way the learning has stayed with each member of our team, and the simple but practical tools have become part of the everyday. Gideon took time to understand our organisation and used relevant examples. Crucially, he helped us see our written communications through fresh eyes. Our writing is now much more considered, not just in terms of audience and message, but how to catch people's imagination and to inspire action."

Corinne Evans, British Red Cross

"I have taken a lot away from this session and already started to make changes to our various case studies and marketing materials. My whole team has come back full of ideas, inspired to improve what we do. I am really excited about the improvements we are going to be able to make to our work incorporating the tips and ideas you have provided."

Sarah Elliott, InKind Direct

Need to develop your charity writing, media or marketing skills?

Introducing one of the UK's leading specialist training providers on charity writing, publications, media skills, marketing and more...

Benefits of working with ngo.media

- **Quick and easy** ways to improve your charity publications and marketing.

- **A practical approach.** You'll learn techniques your charity can use right now, without spending more money or using outside agencies.

- **Charity-specific training and coaching.** Everything you learn is charity focused. Don't waste your time with general training that doesn't apply to your sector.

- **Learn from others.** We've worked with some of the biggest brands in the charity sector over more than a decade. We'll share with you what has worked, and what hasn't, for the nation's most successful charities.

- **Guaranteed results.** Our training will work for you or we'll give you your money back. See specific products for details.

We're continually developing resource to help you and your team improve their communications skills:

- Events
- Training days
- Workshops
- Telephone and online seminars
- Toolkits and learning packs
- Books
- One-to-one coaching
- Coaching groups / circles
- In-house training for your team

We also run the UK's most comprehensive online information resources on charity writing and marketing at www.ngomedia.org.uk

FREE Consultation

For a free telephone consultation with Gideon Burrows, lead trainer at ngo.media, on how we can improve you and your team's communications skills, complete the Contact Us form now at **www.ngomedia.org.uk**